ABOUT SOME HOLIDAYS

AND SPECIAL DAYS

by ALMA KEHOE RECK & HELEN HALL FICHTER

MELMONT PUBLISHERS, INC., Chicago

TABLE OF CONTENTS

Pages

NEW YEAR'S DAY 4

LINCOLN'S BIRTHDAY 6

ST. VALENTINE'S DAY 8

WASHINGTON'S BIRTHDAY 10

MOTHER'S DAY 12

FLAG DAY 15

FATHER'S DAY 17

INDEPENDENCE DAY 18

COLUMBUS DAY 20

UNITED NATIONS DAY 22

HALLOWEEN 24

ELECTION DAY 26

VETERAN'S DAY 28

THANKSGIVING 31

NEW YEAR'S DAY—JANUARY 1

Happy New Year! Happy New Year!
It is the first day of January.
It is the first day of the new year.
Stores and markets and banks are closed.
There is no school on New Year's Day.

We think about the good things
we will try to do in the new year.
We think of ways to do things better.
"Happy New Year!", we say to one another.

LINCOLN'S BIRTHDAY—FEBRUARY 12

February 12 is the birthday
of one of our great presidents.
Hang out the flag!

Abraham Lincoln was born in a log cabin.
He lived on a farm where he worked hard.
He was a poor boy but he became
President of the United States of America.
Lincoln is sometimes called Honest Abe.
He was always fair and kind.
He wanted all the people
to be free and happy.

ST. VALENTINE'S DAY—FEBRUARY 14

It's Valentine Day!
It's Valentine Day!
The postman brings us valentines.
There may be a valentine box at school.
Sometimes boys and girls slip valentines
under the door and run away.

Some valentines are funny.
They make us laugh.
Some valentines are pretty.
They say, "I love you!"

WASHINGTON'S BIRTHDAY— FEBRUARY 22

George Washington was the first president
of our country.
That was more than one hundred years ago.
George Washington was a brave soldier.
He was a good president.
On his birthday, we hang out our flags.

At school, boys and girls read stories
about George Washington.
They learn poems and sing songs about him.

MOTHER'S DAY—

"Happy Mother's Day!" boys and girls say
to their mothers on this day.

"Here is a big hug and a kiss for you.
Here is a present for you, too.
I want to help you, Mother.
I want to help you all I can."

Helping Mother is a good way to say,
"I love you."

Hang out the flag!
Today is Flag Day.
June 14 is the birthday of our flag.

At school, boys and girls may sing
The Star Spangled Banner.
It is a song about the American flag.

Americans are proud of their flag.
Hurrah for the red, white, and blue!

FATHER'S DAY—

THIRD SUNDAY IN JUNE

"Happy Father's Day!" boys and girls say
to their fathers on this day.
"Here is a present for you, Daddy."

Some boys and girls make the presents
for their fathers.
Some buy the presents at a store.

Father's Day is a good day for families
to do things together.

INDEPENDENCE DAY–JULY 4

July 4 is the birthday of our country.
There is a parade on the downtown streets.
Some families may go on picnics.

After dark, there are usually fireworks.
ZOOM! Up goes a rocket!
BOOM! Out come the stars!
Red and green, gold and silver stars
fill the sky.
The Fourth of July is a happy holiday.

COLUMBUS DAY—OCTOBER 12

The world is round, thought Christopher Columbus.
I can sail west
to reach the East.
He sailed west
across the Atlantic Ocean
in three ships;
the *Niña,* the *Pinta,* and the *Santa Maria.*
But he did not reach the East Indies
or India.

Some unknown land got in his way.
This land no one knew about
is where we live.
Columbus had found a New World!

UNITED NATIONS DAY—OCTOBER 24

Peace on earth!
The United Nations tries to keep
peace in the world.
Many nations formed
the United Nations
after World War II.
Each member nation sends men to the meetings.
They try to understand
and help
each other.
They meet in a skyscraper in New York City.

HALLOWEEN—OCTOBER 31

Who-o-o-o! The witches are out!
Boys and girls are ghosts and goblins
on Halloween.
They may wear masks over their faces.
They go from house to house scaring people.

Sometimes boys and girls go to parties
on Halloween.
They bob for apples in pans of water.
They play spooky games.
They tell spooky stories.

ELECTION DAY—
FIRST TUESDAY AFTER
THE FIRST MONDAY IN NOVEMBER

The President of the United States
leads the country.
Citizens over twenty-one
vote for a President
every fourth year.

Voting is private.
No one person sees how another votes.
Votes are counted
at the end of the day.
People watch television
to see who wins.
The President is chosen by the people.

VETERAN'S DAY — NOVEMBER 11

A veteran is someone who has served
in our armed services.
Soldiers. Sailors.
Marines. Air Force men.
Men and women are veterans.
We honor all veterans on this day.
Many whom we honor died
or were injured
fighting for our country.
Uniformed men and women
proudly march in parades.
Flags fly.
Bands play.

THANKSGIVING DAY—

LAST THURSDAY IN NOVEMBER

Many years ago, the Pilgrims
shared a feast with the Indians.
They thanked God for the good
that had come to them.
That was our first Thanksgiving Day.

Now, on Thanksgiving Day, we thank God
for the good things that have come to us.
Many families have big dinners.
They may have turkey and pumpkin pie
for dinner on that day.

Now a resident of Denver, Colorado, Alma K. Reck grew up in the state of Indiana. She was at one time an assistant in the public library at Washington, Indiana, and at Evansville, Indiana. At present, she is a copy writer for a large furniture company in Denver.

Most of Mrs. Reck's leisure time is devoted to writing. Her short stories have appeared in *JACK AND JILL, CHILDREN'S ACTIVITIES*, and *THE CHILDREN'S FRIEND*. She is the author of two books published by Albert Whitman & Company—*THE LOST LITTLE BOY* and *THE WEST FROM A TO Z*.

Mrs. Reck is the mother of a teen-aged daughter.

Helen Hall Fichter, a Nebraskan by birth, now resides in Aurora, Colorado. She holds a Master's Degree in Elementary Education from the State University of Iowa.

Mrs. Fichter has had teaching experience in all grades from the first through the fourth.

In addition to raising a family, Mrs. Fichter finds time to do considerable writing. She has sold stories to *JACK AND JILL, CHILDREN'S ACTIVITIES, THE GRADE TEACHER, THE INSTRUCTOR*, and other periodicals.